# Deborah Sampson

## *Soldier of the Revolution*

by Lee S. Justice
illustrated by Ron Himler

HOUGHTON MIFFLIN BOSTON

Deborah Sampson was born in Plympton, Massachusetts, in 1760. Throughout her childhood, she heard about Boston's Patriots, also called the Sons of Liberty. She heard the talk of independence — of breaking free of Britain.

Freedom was a dangerous and exciting idea. But there was little freedom in Deborah's own life. As she later said, "I was born to be unfortunate."

When she was very young, Deborah's father sailed off on a ship and never came back. Her mother did not have enough money for food. So she decided to look for a family to take her daughter.

Often, poor parents "bound out" a child to another family. In return for a home, food, and clothing, the child would serve the family until age eighteen. Ten-year-old Deborah became a bound servant in the home of the Thomas family of Middleborough.

The Thomases treated Deborah like a daughter. Of course, sons and daughters were expected to work. Mrs. Thomas told Deborah what she should do each day.

First, Deborah had to get up at dawn to begin her household chores. Then, she must help make breakfast for the family. Next, she should feed the chickens and milk the cow. Then, she should water the vegetable garden. After that, she could sew, spin, or weave. Like all farm women, Deborah worked hard.

With the ten Thomas sons, Deborah also hunted and fished. She chopped wood and gathered hay. She did all kinds of heavy work.

Farmer Thomas didn't believe in schooling for girls. But Deborah had always been eager to learn. She already knew how to read and write.

Deborah read every newspaper she could find. A minister gave her a religious book. She soon knew it by heart. She kept a journal. In it, she listed her good actions and her bad ones. She wanted to improve herself.

"I wish you wouldn't spend so much time scribbling," Farmer Thomas complained. But he did not make her stop. So Deborah continued.

At church one day, someone read an important document to the crowd. The document said, "All men are created equal." It said that people had rights — "life, liberty, and the pursuit of happiness." It listed the reasons for breaking free of Britain. At the end of the reading, the listeners leaped up and cheered.

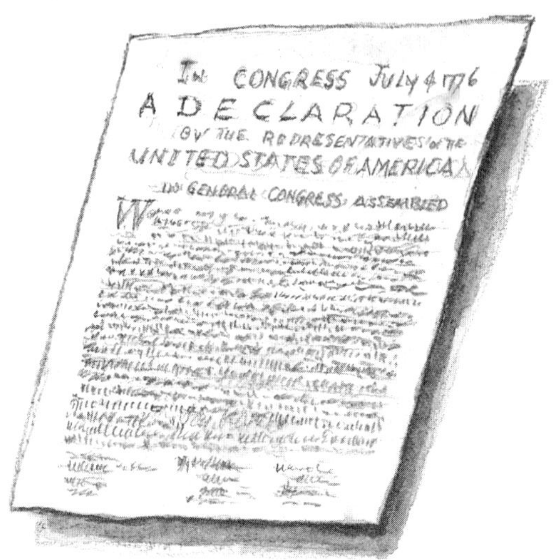


The Declaration of Independence made Deborah's heart pound. But she wondered what some of it meant. She wondered about words like *liberty*.

The soldiers were fighting for liberty. The older Thomas boys had already left home and signed up. Was liberty only for a nation? Or could there be liberty for a sixteen-year-old farm girl?

When she turned eighteen, Deborah began working in people's homes as a weaver. She also taught children for two summers. But by the time she was twenty-one, she was eager for a change.

Deborah had an active mind. She was quiet, but in a strong, confident way. Deborah looked strong, too. And she had grown taller than other women of the time. In fact, she was taller than many men.

But while men her age had a chance to see the world and taste freedom, women didn't. Deborah decided she wanted adventure, too.

One day Deborah's Middleborough neighbors saw her going about her business as usual. The next morning she was gone.

Days later, a young man in farmer's clothes stood before an army recruiter in Bellingham, Massachusetts. "Your age?" asked the recruiter.

"Eighteen," said the young man. His face did not even have a whisker. He looked fifteen, even younger. But the army needed soldiers — young or old. The recruiter did not care.

The young farmer promised to serve for a term of three years. He signed his name: *Robert Shurtlieff.*

Robert Shurtlieff was not a teenage boy. He was Deborah Sampson in disguise.

It was 1782. Fifty new recruits hiked west through the Berkshire hills. Hour after hour, they kept moving without a rest. Deborah, marching among the men, suddenly realized what she had done. She felt terror. If the army found out she was a woman, she surely would be punished. She might be hanged!

Deborah calmed herself. In the days and months ahead, she would have to be watchful. She would play the part of a quiet young man who kept to himself.

After ten tiring days, the recruits reached West Point in New York. There, they received uniforms and weapons. Deborah began training as a foot soldier in the Fourth Massachusetts Regiment.

The war was winding down. But British troops and Tory bands were still active in New York. Deborah joined scouting parties hunting for armed Tories. She faced musket fire. She heard the cries of the wounded. She saw men fall beside her. Luckily, she escaped unharmed.

Then came a morning when Deborah was not so lucky. In a battle with Tories, she was wounded in the head and leg. She begged her comrades not to take her to the hospital. "Let me die here," she pleaded. But they did not listen.

A French doctor at a field hospital treated Deborah's head. She said she had no other wound. The doctor noticed the bloody boot. "Sit you down, my lad," said the doctor, preparing to look at the leg. But Deborah said there was no need.

She secretly tried to remove the musket ball from her own thigh, with no success. The wound would heal, but not fully.

In 1783, Deborah was among the troops in Philadelphia. Sickness spread throughout the city. She became ill. She was brought to a hospital. Her fever was so high that she passed out. When a doctor looked her over, he discovered that the soldier called Robert Shurtlieff was really a girl.

Soon afterward, Deborah Sampson received an honorable discharge from the Continental Army. She returned to Massachusetts.

Deborah Sampson married a farmer named Benjamin Gannett. The couple had three children. They struggled to make a living on their farm.

Years later, Deborah Gannett met a newspaper publisher. He wrote a book based on her life.

The Gannetts worked hard. But they still owed money. In 1802, the newspaper publisher came to Deborah with another idea. How would she like to make money by telling her story to audiences?

In 1802, women did not go on speaking tours. It just was not done. Deborah Sampson Gannett, forty-two years old, thought about the newspaperman's offer. She would have to travel from city to city on her own. She would have to perform before strangers. She would have to memorize a fifteen-page speech.

Deborah said yes. She would do it.

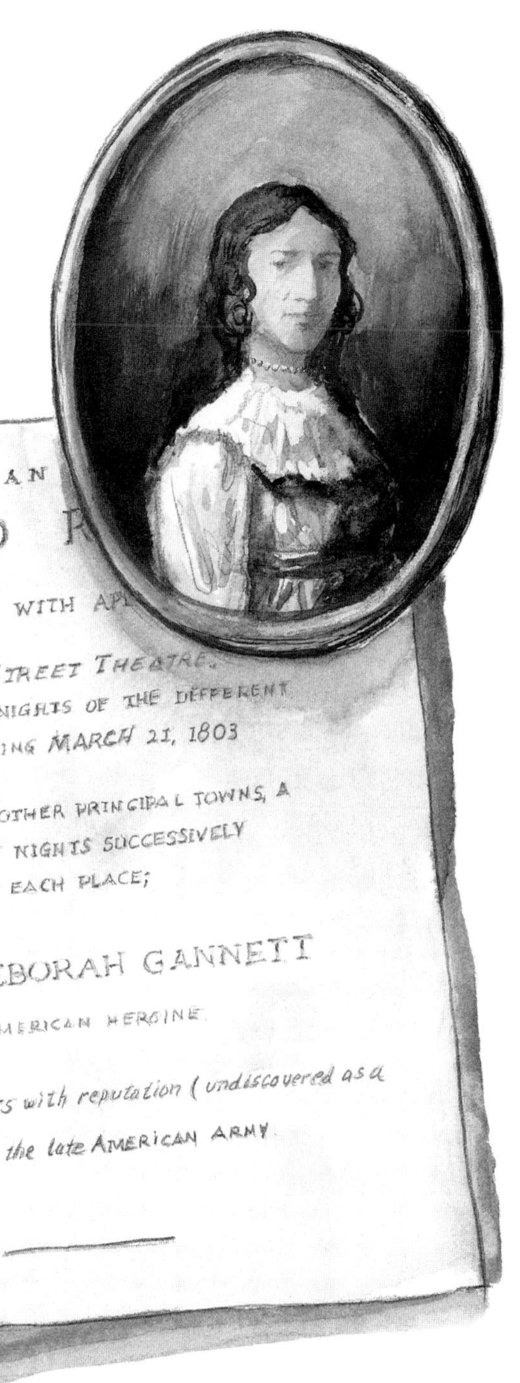
AN
ADD
DELIVERED WITH AP
AT THE FEDERAL STREET THEATRE.
FOUR SUCCESSIVE NIGHTS OF THE DIFFERENT
PLAYS, BEGINNING MARCH 21, 1803
AND AFTER, AT OTHER PRINCIPAL TOWNS, A
NUMBER OF NIGHTS SUCCESSIVELY
AT EACH PLACE;
BY MRS. DEBORAH GANNETT
THE AMERICAN HEROINE
Who served three years with reputation (undiscovered as a
Female) in the late AMERICAN ARMY

Audiences paid to see the unusual soldier. In uniform, Deborah Sampson Gannett performed the drills she had learned as Private Shurtlieff.

She gave her speech in a confident voice. Pretending to be a man was a "bad deed," she admitted. She had taken steps that women were not permitted to take. Terrible memories of the "storms of war" would always be with her. Yet she had done it for the best reasons — liberty and independence.

The new United States government granted small monthly payments to those who had served in the war. Deborah Sampson Gannett was granted payments for her faithful service as a soldier of the Revolution.